You're a Business Owner, Not a Slave

How to Accelerate Profit Growth, Slash Your Work hours and Enjoy a Happier Family Life

An About to Fly Business Book by

Michael Guy Clark

Publishing History

Kindle Edition 1 / November 2018
ASIN: B07KP9LMLY

Paperback Edition 1 / November 2018
ISBN-13: 9781790243822

All Rights Reserved.

Copyright @ 2018 Michael Guy Clark

I wrote this book to make your life easier and you're welcome to share the love. Feel free to pass it on to others, share it, photocopy it, stick it on your wall, put it on your Facebook account, etc., etc. My only request is that when you share these ideas and insights. Let people know where the good ideas came from.

No-Brainer Disclaimer:

This is a book of helpful, general advice. Like all general advice, expect it to be helpful a lot of the time, but never, ever make significant business decisions in your own business without chatting with the experts who specifically know your business inside and out. I take no legal responsibility for decisions that you make in your business. Use your brain, get good, independent advice and give it your best shot.

Books by Michael Guy Clark

About To Fly Business Books

You're a Business Owner, Not a Slave – 2018

Secret Business Growth Strategies – 2018

Table of Contents

Get the Balance of Business Success and Home Life 1
How to Increase Profitability 5
Automate Systems and Processes 14
Effectiveness Beats Productivity in Business 19
The Surprisingly Important KPI 24
Dealing with Competing Priorities 31
Enjoy Home Time with Your Life Partner 34
Dodging the Burnout Bullet in Business..............47
Know Yourself, Your Motives, Fears & Priorities 53
Next Steps: Actions Speak Louder than Plans.....58
Are You Ready to Grow the Next Level? 61

About the Author 64

Get the Balance of Business Success and Home Life

Are you living as a successful business owner or as a tired, helpless slave to your business? Do you have a life outside of your business, or does your work absolutely dominate your time, freedom and family life? This book is designed and custom-built for committed business owners who have been working long hours and fighting hard to build a successful business, but the enjoyment factor of leading your business is wearing off fast. Finally, you are reading a step-by-step, actionable guide to making massive, measurable improvements in both your work and home life.

This isn't a fluffy motivational experience that is meant to wipe away your tears and give you a big, warm hug while inspiring you to go harder. This is a road-map for a path that takes courage and integrity to travel on, and if you aren't willing to face the tough questions that most owners try to side-step, then please stop reading right now and save yourself the time. Initially, it feels easier (and safer) not to make the decisive changes that are necessary to get your life back, but it's the tough choices you make now that will make next year much easier and more profitable than this one.

I'm guessing that some of what you're about to read will be groundbreaking for you. There is already plenty of material out there on how to become a richer business owner. However, that's less than half of what you need to be successful. You also want to balance your work life with having a partner who loves you, kids whom you've got plenty of time for, and your own interests and fun-time outside of work.

A lot of the standard (but irrational) advice out there seems to proclaim that in pursuit of business success you should completely and totally exhaust yourself to generate massive growth in your business, and then go home hoping everything in your home life will work out on its own. You and I, as business owners, know that's not how life works. So, this book encourages you to boldly tackle the challenge of how to be successful both at work and at home. We will look at step-by-step strategies you can implement to ensure your work life and your home life are simultaneously on track. Really, what does anybody gain if they have a fantastic business life and go home to a slowly deteriorating family life? Many of the clients I have worked for have experienced the wild highs of exciting growth at work without knowing how to face the slow-motion train wreck of their home lives. I would suggest that more than half of the clients I work with are facing these issues right now, and some of them are going to experience a lot of pain at home down the track. I don't want you to go through that, so I wrote this guide to make life easier for you.

I want to reassure you that I'm not going to suggest you do more at work. Instead, I'm going to suggest that you need to do less. Aim to reduce your frantic pace at work, squeeze less into your calendar and leave work a bit earlier. Contrary to what most of the herd believe, you're not going to thrive by cramming more activities into your already busy life. In the clear majority of business owners' lives, growth comes at a dangerous, unmeasured cost to people's personal energy, enthusiasm, health and relationships. I know that because I built a business from zero to almost $2 million in annual revenue in a few short years and the cost I paid in my personal life was high. That was a few years ago, but it almost seems like a different lifetime because now my priorities, how I spend my time and the things I do to protect my home life have changed so much. Today, my life with my wife and kids is a great, big, fun adventure, but things would have been a lot easier for all of us if I'd understood the steps you will see outlined in this book.

So, if you've ever wondered if it's possible to get your business thriving and your home life to be enjoyable too, then you are asking the right questions. If you've ever felt guilty about being so successful at work but frustrated at home, then you're ready for positive changes. You're not the only one who has often wondered, "Why is my spouse always annoyed about my work life when I'm wearing myself out to provide for us all?" Also, if you catch yourself thinking, "I wish I could be just an employee again and not be responsible for everything in my business", then you've picked up the right book. Let's go!

How to Increase Profitability

On the road to being a success both at work and at home, certain things have to be bedrock foundations for you. You have to get these things right. First off, and most importantly, you have to be making a healthy profit. Your business has to be succeeding financially. If your business is not making a decent amount of profit and you've been working on it for three years or more, you should seriously consider whether or not it's worth continuing. Think of your opportunities you are giving up in order to stay in your business. After all, you could get a regular job somewhere and earn a reliable wage without all the responsibility and stress you currently carry. Don't find yourself holding onto a non-profitable business just because you have pinned your ego or reputation to it. Either make your business nicely profitable or drop it.

Most businesses are run by people who do not make the important distinction between revenue and profit. Revenue is the money that comes into your bank account. Profits are what you keep at the end of the month. You need to objectively evaluate the likelihood of your business succeeding in the long term, and you do that by looking at the profit, not the revenue. To make things succeed at work, you must be profitable. If you're not making enough that your gross profit margins are at least 10% (sustainably healthy) or better yet 15% (very healthy), then something's broken. You need to be willing to face that because, without those sorts of margins, you will struggle to survive the next downturn that will inevitably come your way. Also, without a reasonable profit margin, your business will lack the budget to get to the point where it can do well without your constant, watchful eye over it.

I'm not asking you to do something I haven't already done because I have made a lot of very hard decisions in my business in the last year or two that meant we lost a lot of clients but made much higher profits. Everyone around me knows these are decisions I absolutely didn't want to make. Yet the irony is that the very same, difficult decisions that were hard on my conscience, and initially caused me a lot of self-doubt and fear were the path that led to my business becoming healthy, profitable and making a substantial income. I've learned from experience that it is less painful to make a tough decision than it is to delay committing to a course of action. My wife used to regularly tell me, "Oh, you look so stressed." She doesn't say that as often anymore because I know things are very much on track at work. We've now got a steady profit coming in each month, and we have plenty of time to relax and enjoy it. Profit is an antidote to stress and fear.

Now if you're sitting there thinking, "It's impossible to quickly turn around my profitability with just a few moves," hold that thought. I'll bet that you can. Here are some things I've done in the last year which helped me do just that, and maybe you can take similar steps.

Increase Your Prices

(Face your fear that all your customers will run away)

I've increased my prices because if I can't make a good profit now, I'm not interested in growing my business at low margins. I can't think of many things more stressful than that. I deliver a fantastic experience for my customers, and I deserve to make a profit. My wife and children deserve to reap the financial benefits that come from the hours I have taken from them and put into our business. Every time we've increased our prices, I've feared we would lose enormous numbers of our customers, but each time, I've been pleasantly surprised when most of our customers have stayed with us. Even when you do lose some customers while raising your prices, you can expect to make higher profits overall because the customers you keep will generate more profits for you, and you will have reduced your cost-base by no longer needing to serve those lost customers.

Change How You Get Paid

(Get paid in advance like clockwork)

We have stopped accepting payments by bank transfer and manual invoice and put all our clients on direct-debit payment systems. Now, our clients' accounts are paid in advance using a direct-debit system, so there's no more money outstanding on people's overdue accounts. Their bank account is automatically debited every fortnight. In implementing this, we lost a few of our most annoying, unreliable customers, but we were surprised by how many of our regularly late-paying customers instantly accepted the new system and became a pleasure to work for. Most direct-debit systems will cost you 1.5%-2% of your revenue in fees which is a very worthwhile price to pay because you earn that back many times over. That's because you will no longer have to spend staff time chasing overdue accounts and because you will never again provide a service that people don't pay for. As soon as we introduced this payment system in our tutoring business, we reduced 12 hours a week of staff time for tracking and following up unpaid accounts.

Stop Pursuing Unprofitable Pursuits

(Drop what isn't working to focus more on what actually makes money)

I shut down two business locations that were unprofitable. We still have ten locations, but each one is making a profit, and I no longer need to support the two locations that were draining our profits. When I decided to shut them down, it felt like a knock to my pride and a knock to our credibility as a team, but it freed up our time and capital to focus on other, more profitable things.

Improve Your Automation and Software Systems

(Well-spent money to improve your systems will increase your profitability for many years to come)

We spent a lot of money to acquire and integrate new software that saved our staff a lot of work and reduced our staff costs. A lot of our work used to be manual such as filling out documents and then passing them on through an old, manual system to give to someone else for approval. Now, we just press a few buttons, and all the necessary steps happen automatically. This is a lot more efficient despite the large amounts of money it cost us to set up. So, one real step to profitability is to streamline your manual tasks by using better software to automate tasks.

Upgrade Your Marketing and Advertising

(Pick the right message to send to the right audience using the right platform)

I used to think I was good at marketing (and I was pretty strong at it), but I outsourced a lot of that role to an expert who cost me what I thought at the time was a lot of money. This move made me five times more in profit than he charged me. Obviously, that is money well spent. Once your business starts to grow, it's a big mistake to continue doing your own marketing.

Most businesses think they are doing a great job of marketing, but they are wasting their marketing budget and missing great opportunities. You must be doing at least an adequate job or your business wouldn't have survived the first two years, but there's always money left on the table when people do their own marketing. Every dollar of marketing money you spend should make you more than a dollar in profit. If there are ways you can do this, and you aren't currently doing it, you are missing real opportunities.

Improve Your Policies

(Stop allowing your clients' poor choices to hurt your profitability)

We also changed a lot of our policies from being very accommodating towards our customers to now being fairer, clearly spelled out and no longer open to interpretation, removing all the "exceptions to the rules" we used to give. In the past, we used to let disorganised customers lead us around, and we bore the inconvenience and the costs of what we were accepting. We don't allow that to happen anymore. Now, with disorganised customers, we say, "Sure, I understand that you faced tricky circumstances, but we still have a well-thought-out, fair policy that we need to stick with." We are gentle but firm.

Find an Outside Set of Eyes

(It's cheaper to pay for quality consulting than it is to continue making the same mistakes)

An insightful consultant costs money, but should always pay for themselves many times over. These ideas for changes to my business didn't come to me in a fantastic dream one night or some flash of insight given to me by an angel. Life doesn't work like that. Instead, we got a lot of help and strategic advice from a consultant and some mentors who have made a huge difference in my business. I keep wishing I had found them years earlier. My consulting team was able to see things my internal team had become blind to and helped boost our profitability to a healthier level. Honestly, I don't think we could have done it without spending the big bucks to get the right advice because objective, external people see through your excuses, and they are willing to prioritise profits over people's feelings (which is harder for a business owner to do).

Most of us fear that if we get firm with our clients, if we raise our prices, if we implement all those changes, then we will lose customers. Those fears hold us back from taking the necessary steps. I hate to be the one to tell you, but if you go out of business in two years' time, your customers are going to be very disappointed. They would much rather have you restructure your business and improve your profitability than not have you there at all! They may not realise this now, but don't show them the hard way by going broke.

Specialise in the Right Niche

(Aim carefully at a specific type of customer, not at everybody)

We all know we need to specialise in something to have that edge over our competitors, but we need to resist the temptation to generate that volume of sales by stepping out of our niche. There is always a segment of the market that is going to be more profitable rather than just aiming right in the middle of the market where you can't stand out as special. If you aim at everybody, you have to charge what everybody else is charging, which probably has very low profitability. My tutoring business ignores the "I'm smart, but I want higher grades" market and specifically targets the "I'm stuck, so build up my confidence and basic skills" market. Also, after a couple of unsuccessful experiments, we have ceased offering home-tutoring and instead only tutor from our premises. Home-tutoring is so competitive that the margins are too thin to be worth the effort. By deliberately ignoring most of the tutoring market, my team can specialise in an area we are very talented in and that I can charge premium pricing for. The greater the problem a customer is experiencing, and the harder it is to solve that problem, the better your niche is and the more you can charge for helping.

If you realise you have drifted from your niche into the mainstream market, or if you've never really chosen a niche, the steps to specialising are straight-forward. First, you decide what type of unusual customer is being under-served by your market but would be willing to pay extra to solve their issues. Then, you change your marketing message to specifically target that type of person. It doesn't mean you can't serve others, but it means you are specifically getting your product or service in front of people with those unusual issues. Then, train your team in those particular skills that the competition lacks. Increase your prices for those clients accordingly.

Make the Necessary Changes

You fear losing customers, and that's a valid concern, but instead of fearing it, simply accept it as an unfortunate outcome of what needs to be done. We've lost some customers because we changed things, but our profitability kept rising. It was totally, absolutely worth it. Plus, guess what? The kind of customers we lost were the ones you don't really want anyway—the ones who are constantly complaining and looking for an extra discount or an exception to the rules. We're much better off without them, and we're much more profitable. Hopefully, they found what they needed elsewhere, but we can't play their games anymore.

It may seem strange to you that I've started this book with such a focus on profitability, but it's something to strive for. Your business needs it like you need oxygen, because if your business is unprofitable or only generating small profits, you will need to put a whole lot more time and energy into sustaining it, and that is unhelpful for having a great home life. Remember, if you can't be profitable, you're probably better off shutting your business down, getting a regular job, and you'll have a much easier, happier life both at work and at home.

Automate Systems and Processes

Your Most Important Work is Building Systems

If you want your work life to be good and your home life to be fulfilling, you need your business to run on systems instead of on you. Your business needs to run like a clock—reliably, predictably and using the same patterns and mechanisms every day. As a business owner, your role is to set up these systems and practices but then let other people drive them.

Many business owners fall into the trap of doing the actual work of their trade. That's a big mistake because every hour you spend doing the work is time that you have not spent building your business strategy, your procedures and policies, or training your key staff.

Some of what you do can be done by setting up systems, processes and policies to get your work done without your input. You also have to quit running your business one decision at a time. Your business needs to be an automatic machine that hums along on its own, only requiring you to be there tweaking it occasionally. I spend more than half my work week perfecting our systems and getting them to work really smoothly.

Fine-tune Customer Service

Most weeks, I will find myself chatting with about three customers. A few years ago I would have chatted with 30 customers each week. However, in the last few years I have instead set up very clear policies for my staff to follow so they can have the conversations I used to have. I've given them the scripts, the tools and the clear-cut boundaries of what we will and won't do for customers. So the only customers I interact with now are ones with really high-level issues or complaints, or when I want to reach out to specific customers to get feedback on new things I want to implement. A lot of business owners fear they will lose touch with what their customers are experiencing and would initially be worried about using this approach, but by ensuring I'm spending at least an hour talking to our customer service team every week, I still have my finger on the pulse of how our customers perceive us. That is just an example, but there are many ways you can stay aware of what it's like "on the ground" without having to live there.

Another thing we've worked on is our phone-call scripts. We systematised what we say to people on the phone and how that information is conveyed to new members of our team. When a new staff member joins us, they only have to go through several sessions of video training to get them ready to go instead of us waiting for weeks until they become valuable.

Automate Everything

We now pay for a lot of software that automates most of our work and much of our interaction with clients. I run a large, successful tutoring business with hundreds of customers. We interact with our clients through email and text messages, and we've drastically improved how we do this. Instead of texting out a two-sentence message, for example, now, we just pull up a specific template on our computer, make a few entries, and with a click of the mouse, there goes the text. We only need to input their name or date, although even that's done for us sometimes. We've applied the same principle to our emails. They're templates arranged by subject. We don't have to think about what we're saying to each parent, we just click on the template we want, and it's done! It took me less than 12 months to smoothly systematise and automate our client communication, but the difference is amazing. It's a lot less stressful for us in the workplace, and our customers are getting a consistent tone and feel in the interactions they have with us by email, texts and phone call.

In the early days, I used to personally train all of our staff. It meant that I could see what skills they needed and I could help them grow their abilities so that we had outstanding, talented staff. Now that we have about 130 staff, that's no longer practical. Instead, we have a series of online videos for staff to build their skills. It works out to be about four, one-hour-long videos that staff members watch during the first couple of months they are with us.

The training starts with basic skills and then over time moves into the harder, more specialised skills that our leaders need to have. We also have a mentoring system set up so new staff receive plenty of help on the job. This process is overseen by one of our most skilled staff members who is excellent at mentoring people, but even if she was to leave us tomorrow, the system is built so that it can be run by anyone. I believe that the whole system took us 200 hours to set up, and has probably already saved us about 1,000 hours of training time. In my industry, I don't know of anyone else who trains their staff in this way, which doesn't make sense to me because I know how much it has helped my business thrive and helped me have time away from work.

So, the real take-home message here is that you need to systematise and automate your business a lot more than you have been. Systems mean you can go home whenever you like and still feel relaxed. I can take two weeks off, and I'm sure things will work out because my systems are properly built. If you build your systems properly, you can go home worry-free, put your phone down, and unwind.

Setting up your business to run without your direct involvement is an enormous task, yet when it is done properly, it is such an effective way of cutting your weekly work hours so you can spend more time at home. Building your business systems is one of the main areas I'd suggest most business owners pay for some outside advice or consulting to get a hand with because every change you make here pays off later. The more effective you can be at automating processes in your business, the more you'll increase profits and save time in the long-term.

To find out more about how we can help you do this in your own business, reach out to us at <u>www.abouttofly.com.</u> **We would love to be a big help to you, and we can also put you in touch with others who can support you.**

Effectiveness Beats Productivity in Business

A lot of people in business these days are talking a lot about the importance of productivity. It's overrated. It's a lot more important to be effective. You can be as productive as you like and have ten lists of things you need to do. At the end of the day, you may have ticked off a lot of tasks, but there's always more to tick off, right? Here's the thing—did you make more money by ticking off each of those tasks? Usually not. So, you can call yourself productive and run around with your list of lists, or you could stop, put the list away, and start your day out differently.

Ask yourself: "What's the one thing I need to do today?" What's the one thing that will have the biggest impact on the profitability, the reputation, the quality, or the marketing of my business? Find your "one thing" and go and do it! It will probably be a challenging, brain-draining thing—a task that takes you a couple of hours because the most important work always takes time. Once you've done that, pull up your list again and do those other things that seem (the key word is "seem") so urgent.

I recently had a business conversation with someone that earned me $25,000 in profit. After I got out of that meeting, I thought, "What else could I do today that could even come close to being that important?" So, I took the rest of the day off! I had achieved my one big thing for that day. This is a great example of being effective rather than productive.

The weird thing was, I had actually put off a lot of other projects earlier in the week to make space for that one, critically important conversation. This was a classic example and lesson to not be focused on being productive but instead to commit to being effective with the one action that had the biggest impact.

Great... Now that we have made the important distinction between being effective and being productive, let's move onto the smaller issue of productivity.

Use Work Time Wisely

Are you ready for some strategies to significantly grow your personal productivity? Most of the emails I send are three-liner emails. I don't deal with customers often in my emails. My admin staff takes care of that. My emails are for people I'm collaborating with on projects. Three lines—type, type, type, send, gone.

Often when I'm travelling in the car during my work hours, I'll be phoning a staff member. I could be coaching someone, leading someone, or planning with someone while I drive, because driving time is also my phone call time. I have to be in the car, so I might as well use that time effectively.

Phone Call Tips

I never ask someone to call me at a specific time; I call them. That way I'm not sitting around waiting around for them to be ready. I will agree with them that "I'll call you at three." If I'm a bit late, I'm calling at five past three, that was their time spent waiting for me, not my time spent waiting for them.

On the subject of phones, add everyone who calls you as a phone contact, so, when they call you, you know who's calling. Play out this scenario: Phone rings. You look at the number. You don't recognise it so you pick it up thinking it may be important. It's not. You spend the next five or 10 minutes racking your brain about how to get off the phone.

That doesn't happen to me. When I pick up my phone, I know exactly who it is. If it's some random person or I don't remember them by name, I'll record it in my phone contacts as "demanding customer [name] complains about [issue]". That's their name on my phone, so when they ring, I can see it and think, "Yeah, I'm not taking this call right now. I'll deal with it later." Having every number as a contact in your phone will give you lots of leverage with your time because you won't be picking up the phone at times that don't suit you.

I don't like to enter the business zone when I'm at home with my family, and this one habit of entering every single contact into my phone so that I can always know who's at the other end of the phone means I never have to accidentally answer the phone at home for a low-priority business issue.

Work from Home

When you are doing really challenging, strategic work, don't do it at your office or workplace. Pick a regular day and time each week when your spouse and kids won't be there, and get stuck into the most important strategic work you have. That's because you can't think effectively when you have the usual work distractions around you. Instead, do your hardest work at home where you can focus and work most effectively. I work from home most of the time, and I go to the office enough to keep my finger on the pulse, but I don't try to do hard work there. At a minimum, do one day a week at home. If you want to get real traction and progress in your business, work two days a week from home.

In fact, I've seen the results for business owners of getting away from the office to do their hardest work, and I'm so convinced by what I've seen that even my "Office Manager" works from home a day each week now. Have you ever heard of an "Office Manager" who worked from home? Yet that's what has driven so much positive change in our business.

Do Tasks in Batches

I've learned that "batching tasks" is a key. Do the same kinds of tasks all at once—like this book. Do you think I wrote a chapter a week? No, my team and I sat down and hammered the whole thing out in about two weeks because we then had inspiration, flow and drive. I didn't drag it out for months. Most tasks you do at work are like that. You can batch similar tasks together or tackle big tasks by giving them a big chunk of time. You can get things done much more efficiently than if you do everything in bite-sized pieces.

Know the Next Step

Here is a tip for working with people which you, as a business owner, inevitably should aim for. At the end of a conversation, ask the person you're speaking with, "What's the next step?" They'll tell you, "Oh, the next step is I need to do this," or "The next step is you need to do such and such." And then ask, "What's the next step after that?" And they'll tell you. Make sure it's written down. Then agree with them, "Great. Let's make that happen by such and such a date." It shortens meetings, especially most face-to-face meetings, by about 20-50%.

The productivity ideas I've shared with you, as well as others you can find online, are helpful, but they won't change your work life. They're not going to make you a success both at work and at home. A "success", as I use the term in this book, is someone whom people look up to, someone who has a positive impact, someone who is very effective when they choose to spend their time on the important things, someone who loves their life. Let's look at how you can make that happen.

The Surprisingly Important KPI

To be a success in both your work life and your personal life, you have to know when to work and when to stop. I used to struggle with that and only got the hang of it in the last couple of years. Nowadays, I'm working about 30-35 hours a week. That's it. I'm not interested in working more than that because there are no real, long-term benefits from it. I realised I could double the amount of time I put into my work, but that would increase my profit by only about 10%. What a waste of my life, right? Be honest with yourself. If you're working more than 45 hours a week, that needs to change. It's not sustainable, and you're not getting good value for your overworked hours. If you can't get it done in 45 hours, it really isn't going to have a huge impact on your business.

Reducing my work hours was really difficult because I had fallen into the trap of believing that hard work and long hours are virtuous. They aren't. They are just a sign of ineffectiveness. To help myself break this pattern, I measured my daily work hours so I could make a graph of them in a spreadsheet at the end of each week. Then, I could see patterns and trends. I noticed that I tended to have a very short work day on Mondays and a very long day on Tuesdays. Then, my work hours usually went back to normal for the rest of the work-week. Armed with this up-to-date information, I could limit my work hours further when I want to. I tracked my work hours for about nine months while I reduced my work time from 55 hours down to 40 hours each week. Whenever I noticed that for a week or two in a row I was working more hours than I'd like, I could change that because I was tracking it and aware of it. Every couple of months, I track my work hours for two or three weeks at a time just to check that I'm not getting back into patterns of working long hours again. Remember, what you measure (including your work hours), you can manage and change.

80/20 Your Work

I met another business owner about six months ago when I was travelling, and his out-of-control life was a very helpful lesson for me. He told me he works 90 hours a week. Seriously? That's more than double what I work, so I asked him, "Why?" As a consultant who helps people get their work hours under control, I was extremely interested in why he spent 90 hours a week working. Once he described what he does each week to me, everything made sense. It was clear that his business was profitable but wasn't built on systems. It was built on him, which kept him "trapped"—completely tied to his business.

He described how so many different projects in his business happened at the same time and he had to run them all. He couldn't focus on one thing, complete it, and move on. Also, he had delegated a lot of low-level work to his staff, but he had never equipped or authorised them to do the more challenging work, so he was the one who had to do that.

Here's what he just did not understand: if you focus on the important things, and build systems for the lower-impact tasks, you will drastically reduce your work hours. This is the Pareto principle, the 80-20 concept. This means 80% of your results come from the most important 20% of your efforts. To harness the power of 80-20, we need to ask ourselves, "Where am I going to put my time and effort to have the biggest impact?" "What are the main things I'm going to do to have a big impact on the health and long-term profitability of my business?" Unfortunately, this guy had never done that.

Let the side projects fall to the side or even forget all about them. They're not making you most of your money. What makes you money is doing the few, most important things. To really do well and for sustainable, healthy business growth, do those high-impact, carefully chosen tasks to a high standard.

Delegate Strategically

There's a lot of talk about the need for business owners to delegate, but few people do it effectively. Some of it simplifies reality and isn't helpful because you have to be very selective about what to delegate. There are some things you could delegate quite easily and others you shouldn't delegate at all. Some things are not constructive for you to delegate. I'm a business owner and CEO. I run Big Improvements Tutoring, and I feel particularly committed to it because I also founded it. It generates almost $2,000,000 gross revenue each year. I can't just delegate my marketing to someone. My marketing is too important. The message of my marketing is something I've been crafting for the past five years. I know what the market needs to hear, and I can't just tell some random person, "Hey, you! I'm going to pay you some money. Do my marketing for me." It doesn't work like that because they don't know what I know about how my market will hear their messaging, and it's unreasonable for me to expect them to have that knowledge.

So, how do we get that work done without consuming too much of my time? Well, I can outsource most of my marketing tasks by paying someone to do the mechanics of it—putting up ads, figuring out how much to spend, getting a graphic designer, etc. Sure, but I can't outsource the creation of the message. The core message should come from me or someone in my business who understands it wholeheartedly.

So, what can most business owners successfully delegate? Our accounting? Our graphic design? Most business owners don't know how to delegate properly. Why is that? We fear delegating to others because we already know they won't do the job as well as we would (and we are often right—others can't do the tasks as well or carefully as we could). However, we fail to consider that if we don't delegate tasks to them, we're going to have to keep doing the task which will take us away from the things that have a bigger impact on our profitability. So, delegating and outsourcing is another key to becoming a success at work and at home. Otherwise, you're at work micromanaging everything (because you didn't get rid of what you should have), or you're at home thinking about all the things you didn't finish at work (because you're too busy micromanaging everything). If you're not willing to start delegating just a little bit more than you think should be delegated, then you will be trapped in your job. That's because while you are busy setting up systems to hand off some of your work, your business continues to grow and change. So we need to transfer as much of our work onto our team as we can reasonably quickly, so we can then pass off more of the new work that lands on us while we're doing that. Anything that can be delegated should be, and, if in doubt, delegate more rather than less.

Once you start to delegate, you can't just drop responsibility for what you have passed to others and stick your head in the sand. It is still your role to oversee things, especially in the early days while others are building up their skills. Delegate tasks to specific people who have the right skills (or to whom you can teach the skills) and then keep track of those tasks by checking in with those people at set dates and keeping them on that particular timeframe. When things are going wrong, you will see it early, and you can deal with any problems. Then you can help your team build systems so that one day if they are no longer doing that task for you, someone else can pick up the system and learn it more quickly than they did.

Be aware of when you're working. I get most of my best work done between 5 a.m. and 7 a.m. No phones are ringing, there's nothing that needs my attention, and my kids and wife are asleep. It's the perfect time of the day to get things done. Another productive time (occasionally—not regularly) is between 10 p.m. and midnight for the same reasons, as long as I have a coffee first.

I spend my afternoons picking up my kids from school, my evenings hanging out with my wife and kids at dinner, and when they head off to bed, I can knock out some work without any distractions. Nothing is competing with me and keeping me from working on the important tasks. I'm not advocating that everyone should work until midnight. For some that would be disastrous. Those are just my peak times: 5-7 in the morning and 10-12 at night. I still work during the day. I'm just not as effective as I am in my peak hours.

Try to come up with peak times that don't impact your family. My wife doesn't care if I'm working at 5:30 a.m. She's asleep and so are my kids. Finding times that work for your whole family is a positive step towards feeling like a real success at home.

When it comes to balancing entrepreneurship and family, I think it's crucial to be very clear about when we're working and when we're not. Sometimes when I'm at home on a Friday afternoon, my kids might ask, "Is Dad working, or is he hanging out?" The boundary isn't always clear. They want my attention, but I'm sort of pushing them away. In this situation, I say to them, "Hey guys, I'm at work. I'll probably be at work for two more hours, but I should be free after that." By saying that, I set a boundary that enables them to know what's going on. They're not going to be confused thinking, "Oh, what's wrong with Dad? He doesn't seem to be very warm at the moment."

The barriers stopping people from limiting their work hours are usually related to a lack of systems in place or a lack of delegating to others. We need to be profitable in order to start paying others to work for us, so, we must work hard to establish our profitability, and then we have to work hard to develop our systems. Only then can we take a deep breath because we can massively reduce our work hours and spend a whole lot more enjoyable time at home with our spouse and children. Sure, it is a process, but most business owners who are just starting out in doing this should be able to make a noticeable impact in just a couple of months and really cut big chunks out of their workload well within a year. How fast you go on making progress with this is largely up to your own commitment to getting your life back, and whether or not you have a business that is profitable (and worthy of pursuing) to start with.

Are you ready to make some real changes in your business? Then remember to check out the resources at www.abouttofly.com**.**

Dealing with Competing Priorities

Know What Matters Most

Being on track at work and at home requires you to prioritise. I don't just mean thinking, "Task A is important versus Task B which is not important." For everything that comes across your desk, you want to be able to look at it and assess **"How important is this?"** What is its rank on the scale? I've got three levels: Level 1 (highest), Level 2 and Level 3 (lowest).

> Level 1: Focus on it – it matters so much!
>
> Level 2: Get to it soon.
>
> Level 3: Necessary, but not valuable.

What's Level 1? This is the level of things that need to be done today, the "now" issues. They significantly affect profitability, long-term viability, or your enjoyment of your home life. These might be a work task, like a project that's too important and can't wait another day, or it could be my daughter's birthday party. I have to go; I'm a dad. Those are Level 1 issues for me.

Level 2 issues are things that are also important but do not reach a Level 1. They are significant but not a "now" issue. They can wait until tomorrow. If one of my staff members wants to have a chat with me about something that is pretty important to them, it's not something I want to overlook. I'll schedule them in for the next day. It's not a "now" issue. It's not going to be more important than time with my wife and kids. It can wait. I'm not going to treat Level 2 issues like Level 1 issues.

Then comes everything else: Level 3—the things you need to complete. The forms that need filling out. The tax forms, the insurance forms, the things that you can't "not do", but...they can wait. As soon as you start prioritising things as Level 1, Level 2, or Level 3 issues, then you become very clear about how you should spend your time. You stop responding to the demands of others. A lot of your customer issues are Level 3 issues that could be dealt with by someone else. They don't even need your time at all, and you just send a quick message delegating it to someone else to contact so-and-so and solve whatever the drama is. You've just saved yourself 20 minutes. Gone, solved, and yet the customers will still be happy.

Keep Things in Perspective

I used to think every issue was a Level 1 issue until I started being very conscious about distinguishing between how important issues actually were. I think it's because human beings are designed to respond to threats. If you go back to the caveman days when you had to hunt for meat to feed your family, there were always threats around. You always had to look out for danger. As business owners, we're wired to look for threats too, thinking, "Where's the threat? What's the next one going to be? I've got to make sure everything is okay." Here's the antidote I use. I literally say out loud to myself, "Where is your confidence? Today's threat will be forgotten in 6 months." Get confident, get secure and know that your business is strong enough to survive any threat. Then start thinking rationally about what level of importance the issues you are facing really are.

Having a prioritisation system, being able to see what issues are Level 3, will help fight your instinct that everything is a threat. Most of the things you're facing are not threats. Even if they appear on the surface to be a threat, they're not a **real threat.** They don't need to be dealt with today, and more of them than you think probably don't need to be dealt with by you.

To find out more about how you can do this in your own business, please visit our website at www.abouttofly.com.

Enjoy Home Time with Your Life Partner

I don't think you want to be single twelve months from now. If you're currently married or in a long-term relationship, you don't want your success at work to cause failure at home. I've learned a lot working with people and being a consultant about what can work and also what doesn't work, won't work, and can never work in the future. Let me share what I've seen to save you some heartache. Obviously, there are exceptions to every generalisation, and you may be one of them, but here are some home truths that I keep seeing in the relationships of business owners I work with.

Tips for Business Men

When I chat with women about how their husbands are doing at work, these are the kinds of things I'm hearing. They keep telling me their husbands or boyfriends don't hear them when they are talking. In practice, this means the husband comes home emotionally drained at the end of a busy day, and he's not fully tuned in to his wife. When he is listening to her talk with him, he's not realising that her objective is to connect emotionally, so he is offering practical solutions she wasn't asking for. What does this all this mean? When women are talking to their husbands about their day, they're not looking for solutions. They don't want their husband to solve the drama for them. Most male business owners think that if they solve the issue their wife is presenting, then she will then go back to being happy, and they can get on with their evening. It doesn't work like that. Most businessmen (who are accustomed to solving problems at work all day long) are completely unaware that their spouse is telling them about the dramas of her day so that he can share in the experiences of her day.

When we understand the purpose of that conversation, the interaction is much smoother. So, a major tip for guys—don't solve it. Just listen and be empathetic. It's super easy when you understand the purpose, but impossible until someone lets us in on the secret.

As we come home after serving people at work all day, we don't have much to give, and yet, the heart-cry coming from your wife or girlfriend is, "Tell me I'm special. Tell me I'm important to you. Where have you been all day? Tell me I'm important to you." Now, it's hard for us because we come home and almost always view that as her weakness or neediness, thinking "Why are you like that?" She needs what she needs, and to her, it's not being weak or needy—it's just connecting. She's special, she's important, and listening to her is something that lets her feel valued. She'll be happier, and your relationship will be stronger if you understand her better and are able to give her what she needs.

The last thing for men to be aware of is that hearing feedback from our women is difficult. When she's talking about how you should be different, it's hard to hear that as just feedback. We hear that as a complaint, and then we respond defensively. If we learned to take feedback for what it is, just as feedback and not taking it as personally, our home life would be a lot easier.

Tips for Business Women

Many women who are business owners come home with all the buzz of the workday going through your head, feeling slightly overwhelmed by all the tasks you face at home and look forward to connecting emotionally in conversation with your man. So, it's important for you to know that most days when it comes to his listening abilities, your husband or partner is not ready for a real conversation during the first 15 minutes when he gets through the door because he is turning up at home with an emotionally depleted tank. Give him 15 minutes to do whatever he needs to, whether it's busying himself in the kitchen or just being lazy and sitting on the couch. If you give him the 15 minutes before you go to him with your personal needs, life will be a lot easier for both of you. He'll have the energy to support you, and you're more likely to get your needs met.

It's difficult but worthwhile. I talk with a lot of women who deal with this. It's very hard to hold back from chatting about your day and hanging out with him because it's what feels natural. It's what builds your connection. It's important to understand that he wants to serve you by connecting with you in conversation and he wants to give you what you need, but he struggles to do that in the first 15 minutes. So just give him 15 minutes when he gets home, and you'll find out that he's almost a different guy.

Time Together

It's important for us to set time aside specifically for spending with each other. In work life, there are always demands that come up which appear to be urgent. At least they always sound important, they become the main priority, and our marriage or our relationship becomes a lower priority. On some days, it will just have to be like that, especially if your business is not yet built on effective systems, but it doesn't have to be like that every day.

I highly recommend having a date night at least once a week. Really? Every week? Most people will look at me incredulously and say, "I couldn't do that! How will I get a babysitter? How could I spare the time?" Well, let's think about this for a moment. You're an entrepreneur who simultaneously deals with staff, clients, profitability and a million other things, but you're telling me that you can't organise a babysitter? Really? You're a business owner who pays your staff the big bucks, and you can't afford to pay the next-door neighbour's daughter a few dollars to babysit your kids? Are you kidding me? Seriously? I think the truth is that people don't understand the value of a regularly scheduled date night, so they don't make sure it happens.

When I tell most people that my wife and I have a date night every week, they look at me like I'm from another planet, yet they always say they wish they could do that themselves. It's not as hard to make happen as people think it is. My wife and I have been doing that pretty much every week for the last twelve years, and the impact on our marriage has been terrific. I would never go a week without it.

We need to **specifically create the time with our spouse, cherish it, and protect it.** If we don't, then we are missing the point of why we are working so hard. We are missing out on life. My wife and I also try to have a coffee each week sometime during the day. I find it a bit harder to get in the zone with her because in the middle of the day my focus is going off with all the projects I'm working on. It's much easier for me after work. Figure out what works best for you.

You got together for a reason. You got together for a reason, and you want to hang out together because that probably matters a lot more to you than your business. At least, one would hope it does. The consequences of your business failing compared to the consequences of your home life failing are in different leagues.

Boundaries of Work Life and Home Life

What about those of you who work with your partner? I know a lot of business owners who do. I work with my wife, so when we come home, when does work stop and home life begin—especially since I work from home most of the time? She's at the office, but I work at home a lot, and so, if it's 5:31 p.m., does that mean we're not at work? Here's an example—Let's imagine that I receive a text message request on my phone at 6 p.m. from a staff member wanting to set up an important transaction before she goes home. It's something little that my wife could do in one minute. So, I go to my wife and say, "Could you please do this now for her?" All of a sudden I've turned home life into work life. Sometimes it is worth it, but if you need to do that, be aware of what it is costing your relationship.

Also, after you have stepped into "work mindset', you have to revert back to home life mode. You need to find a way for both of you to step back into your "home mindset'. I don't want to suggest any particular ground rules because inflexible rules don't work, but what is necessary is a **method of communicating with each other about when you're in "work mode" and when you're "at home'.**

When can your spouse feel totally relaxed around you instead of worrying that you'll be checking your phone to deal with some drama or to protect yourself from tomorrow's issues? It's tough. If you're working with your spouse, it's even harder, but there are ways to make things work most of the time. So it's critical that both you and your partner can come up with a way to clearly delineate when you are working and when you are with your family.

Avoid Absent-parent Syndrome

Everyone wants to avoid risking their kids growing up and saying, "My dad was never home because he was always working, so he never had time for me." I find this issue quite difficult because like all parents, I wish I was more available to my children, and I hold myself to pretty high standards.

Sometimes I'm travelling for work and away overnight. Sometimes I'm working on the weekend. There are some weeks when I can take all of Wednesday off, but on Saturday, I've got to get things ready for the following week. It's hard to enjoy your work when you feel like you are neglecting your family.

When I'm going through a busy work time and my hours are temporarily spiking upwards, I make time for my kids individually. I deliberately take just my son or just my daughter out for a coffee. My kids are eight and six. My little boy likes hamburgers; my little girl likes decaf coffee—she's a coffee girl (could it be her mum's influence?). Taking my children out one-on-one is called a "Dad date." I sit there with my child, I listen, and I stay off my phone. This lets them know that they're valued.

So, when things at work need sudden attention or when work is scheduled at a time that affects my kids, and I have to say, "Look, I can't play now. I can't hang out now," my kids still hear the disappointing "No", but they don't forget about the other times when we have a "Dad date". Each "Dad date" matters. It's on top of the time I play with both of them at home. It's something super-special that really puts a smile on their faces and helps me develop a healthy relationship with them. I really recommend scheduling times like this in your diary because unless it's in your diary, it's not going to happen by itself.

Another way I've tried to ensure my children don't resent my work is by telling them the reasons **why** I'm doing it. Why am I going to work? I'm travelling a bit for work because I'm the owner of Big Improvements Tutoring, and we help about 600 families in 10 locations. I'm also one of the key leaders at About to Fly which is a consultancy helping business owners get their work life and business profitability on track. So, sometimes I have to be away. When I go away, I say to both of my kids before I go, "I need to go. I'll be back tomorrow night when you're in bed. I'm going to earn money so that we can have more pizza nights out and spend more time together."

My kids both say, "Oh, I'd rather you didn't go, Dad, but I know it's worth it." They know the **"why'; they know that I am not just disappearing**. They understand that I am going to generate income for the family and that makes it easier for them. We aim to have a family night once a week which is why I can say that. My wife and I, with our kids, watch an animated movie while we eat home delivered pizza. It's deliberate family time, and it happens regularly. It's healthy and fun, and it keeps work from taking over our lives.

Family pizza nights in—they're joy, they're fun. I love to sit there with my little boy on my left side and my little girl on my right. My wife will usually be lying down on the couch. It's just a happy time, and there's no effort required. I sit there enjoying pepperoni pizza, my brain switched off, laughing at a harmless kids' show and everyone around me is happy. Creating those happy family routines balances the time when I have to say "no" to my wife or kids.

Sometimes, as business owners, we become too focused on ticking off all the things on our to-do lists. Your home life shouldn't be one of them. **There should be joy in your home life.**

Here's something else I deeply believe in, and when I first explain it to my friends, they usually find it surprising and unusual. But after hearing the reasons why it works, they often adopt it in their own lives. You are going to have those times where you're jam-packed at work for a week or so with some long days, and you're not going to spend the time with your family that you want to. Times like that happen to everyone. Should you spend your very limited time with your wife or with your kids? When I have to make that choice, I **always, always, always choose to spend time with my wife** because I know that my relationship with my wife is more important in the long-term than my relationship with my kids. In practice, a lot of the time gets spent as our family (all of us) together, but I'm particularly focused on my wife's needs over my children's needs.

Here's why: When I'm away, my kids can still have their emotional needs met by my wife—she compensates for me when I'm gone. When my kids grow up and leave home, I'll still be in a loving relationship with my wife, and so she's my primary focus. I figure if my marriage is healthy, then my kids are getting a good deal.

The alternative when I have limited time would be that I could spend that time with my kids instead of my wife. Then, in five years' time, I might be divorced. Look at the statistics to see how frequently people grow apart. I just don't think it's a risk I want to take. In no way am I suggesting for people to proactively ignore their kids all the time and choose their partner over them in every scenario. I'm speaking only of those really difficult weeks where your time away from work is minimal.

You and I don't want to be known as absent parents who didn't care enough. Frankly, no sane parent wants that. The reality is that every parent raises their children to the best of their ability and every child grows up and complains about how their parent wasn't there for them in those couple of crucial, life-changing moments.

We're just doing our best. As a dad, I'm a limited resource. Twice a week I pick up my kids from school. Most dads don't get to do that, but there are other things my family will miss out on because of the responsibilities of owning a business. By accepting that my time and energy are limited resources, it takes some of the pressure off myself. I wish that I could be perfect as a dad, but I just know that is not going to happen. What really matters is whether or not we can look at ourselves in the mirror and feel proud that despite our imperfections, we are doing a pretty good job of raising our kids.

All these factors mean it's important for family-oriented owners of businesses to make sure they get the balance of work life and home life right. After all, we want the best for our kids, not to become another "absent parent" statistic.

A Personal Invitation from Michael

Congratulations!

You have my personal respect because you have read through some of the toughest sections of this book and you have hung in there, and you are clearly committed to growing your business and getting your life back. That puts you in the 10% of business owners who are willing to make real changes in their business, instead of the 90% who talk the talk but don't walk the walk.

That's why I'd love to invite you to come and get some value from About To Fly. It's easy—just go to www.abouttofly.com to book a FREE 20-minute strategy session. The right strategy will lead to the right results. Your session might be with me, or I might introduce you to another member of my team (depending on what your business actually needs).

You'll notice that I didn't tell people about this invitation in the early chapters of the book because I only want to work with people who are committed and who have "stickability" in their character.

So, what have you got to lose? How could you pass up an invitation like that?

Let's make some positive changes happen before you even continue to the next chapter. Jump on www.abouttofly.com take a minute to contact me there.

Dodging the Burnout Bullet in Business

We face limits, and we can't do everything we want to because we have finite resources of time and energy. If we don't look after ourselves properly, then we're going to struggle in our business life and in our home life. I often feel that people's time goes in three main directions (or focus areas).

1. Your business
2. Your family
3. Your personal self

It would appear that the first focus of my life is my business and the things I have to do to make sure it's working properly. The second is my home life—I make sure my wife and kids are happy, on-track and that I'm looking after them in the ways I need to. Then, the third focus area in my life is my personal time — also known as "me time."

A lot of business owners tell you that "Oh, my family comes before my business," but I think in practice that's just not how life works. Yes, your family is more important to you than your business, but if your phone or email system at work suddenly goes down, or if your biggest client is suddenly quite unhappy and wants to talk with you today to solve things, you are usually going to prioritise those issues over what you had planned with your family. This does not mean that you are failing to prioritise your family relationships. It just means that you are like every other business owner—just doing whatever it takes to keep things working so you can enjoy your family time and your personal time.

When I'm short of time, the first thing that gets cut is "me time." It's the easiest thing to cut out for a short period. We can sleep a bit less, skip grabbing lunch with friends, reduce exercise time, etc. When work is demanding more time from me, I cut out socialising and take that time that's normally reserved for myself and give it to my family or work.

For a while, that is okay, but in the longer term, it's an ineffective Band-Aid solution. It's not going to pay off after a couple of weeks because it really isn't sustainable. To your business, you are an asset. If your business is not yet set up on good systems and practices, you are probably the most important asset to your business. You wouldn't mistreat an asset at work, would you? You wouldn't throw your computer on the floor, or burn down your building. They are assets; you look after them. You are an important asset in your business. You need to look after yourself.

If you've just founded a start-up, you can expect to be short of spare time. Your business is effectively like a helpless little baby that frequently needs its nappy changed and needs feeding and micromanaging

For a season, that's okay but it can get out of control, and I learned that the hard way. There were times where I spent all my time at work, not looking after myself, not eating properly, failing to exercise, and one day I even found myself in the back of an ambulance because I'd pushed myself too hard and not looked after myself physically.

That was a wake-up call, so I had to turn my priorities around. My self-care is on track now, so I've got time to play sport regularly, read about two books each week and just take life easy some days.

I made hard decisions to put systems in place, and I made sure my profitability at work was healthy enough that my physical presence there was less required. Sometimes, you need to work hard in the short term to get a break in the long term.

There are three main areas of our personal life and time that need to be on track for us to thrive and avoid burnout:

1. Relational-social—the "social me";
2. Health aspect—the "healthy me";
3. Emotional/spiritual aspect—the "deep me".

Keeping Socially Healthy

For the relational-social aspect in your family, most of what you've been reading so far in this book covers that. But outside your family, the first thing that business owners cut corners on is usually their socialising time—spending time with friends. Do you often find yourself saying to friends, "Yeah, sorry, it's just a really busy week, I'll catch you guys next time"? Try to minimise that. It's important to have things to look forward to. If you don't have those things, some part of you isn't healthy, and your motivation and effectiveness will both suffer.

Staying Physically Healthy

People struggle to allocate time to attend to their health—their diet and their physical fitness. As soon as you're working 50 or 60 hour weeks, your fitness just goes out the door, and we all know how easy it is to start putting weight on when work is super-busy. Don't let your health slide. Remember to prioritise your exercise time, eat well, and get a good night's sleep. If you can't find time to do these normal human functions, then you need to question whether or not your business is worth pursuing. It's not worth sacrificing your life for.

Your Emotional-Spiritual Health

Then there's the emotional or spiritual part of you; the part of you that connects on some sort of deeper level to more than just the physical, more than just the here and now. I feel like we often ignore that part of ourselves almost to our own peril. To stay in the game of business in the long-term though, you need to be deliberately building that part of yourself. Everyone needs an internal compass to navigate life with – to know why you are taking certain actions and to help you decide and act on your priorities. That deeper emotional and spiritual part of you is where you draw the stamina and purpose for the work you have ahead of you. I don't know what will work for you, but I do know that for me, I know who I am, I know Who my God is, and I know what He's put me here to do. That gives me a lot of stability. I've met very few people who don't attend to the spiritual-eternal-quiet part of themselves who carry a deep, clearly visible sense of peace. I think that's because there is a real sense of emptiness and futility that comes from being completely focused on achievements or material things, rather than on who you are deep down or on the bigger purposes of life.

Enjoy Your Life

So, give yourself permission to go and watch that new movie you've been looking forward to seeing. Fun times are really important because you have to keep life in balance.

You look around at your business-time needs, your family-time needs, and then you look at your self-care-time needs. Constantly sacrificing the other areas of your life for your business is not a good idea. Being a martyr for your business is neither healthy nor virtuous. When you are slaving away at your business, it's simply an indicator that you have lacked the foresight to set up your business to run without you. Take it as a well-timed warning sign and make some changes. Structure your business properly, fix your profitability, set up some systems, document your procedures, and then get out of the way. That's a much healthier approach. That's where you want to be aiming. If you're not there yet, that's okay, but set some plans in motion.

To get some specialised help to learn how you can do this in your own business, get in touch at www.abouttofly.com.

Know Yourself, Your Motives, Fears & Priorities

Dare to Ask Hard Questions

Are you ready to go exploring some uncharted territory in your own mindset and outlook? It will be simultaneously challenging and worthwhile. This is not a comfortable book—it's a results-focused book—and you only get the results from putting in the strategic, difficult work. It's critical that you dig deep to know yourself and your own motives. Why are you putting so much time and energy into your business? Why are you so worried about home? Is something stressing you? If you know what drives you, you can make better decisions.

So, if I look at my work life, here is what I saw two years ago when our tutoring business was significantly less profitable than it is now. The systems weren't quite built properly. There were a lot of unsatisfying, frustrating, routine issues constantly cropping up and demanding my attention each week.

Face Your Fears

I think the true reason why I was micromanaging things in my business so often was because I felt insecure and worried about customers leaving me, so I kept over-accommodating them and creating exceptions to our usual ways of doing business. A large part of me was insecure, and an even larger part of me feared failure. In fact, I even got to the point where I thought, "This is crazy! I would rather have my business collapse and be forced to go and work for someone else than keep working long hours in a stressed environment." Enough was enough!

Once I understood the insanity of what I was doing , I found the courage to change. I owned it. I have a fear of failure and a fear of looking stupid. My big fear is that I'm going to fail, look stupid, and when I walk down the street, people whom I hardly even know will stop and stare at me and say, "Oh, that's the guy who used to be my boss—but he turned out to be a real fake and a loser." At the bottom of it, that's my fear.

Find What is Driving You

Another thing I've come to see in myself is the seemingly never-ending drive to grow my business and demonstrate to "the whole world" that I have what it takes to succeed. Unless I face this immature desire head-on, I will always be hard-driven, always working furiously towards the next big thing. I'd never stopped and thought

"How much success is enough? How much income is enough?"

Instead, I've always thought (without asking why):
- "I want to be more successful."
- "I want to make more money."
- " I want to grow my business."
- "I want to influence and help more people."

The desire to grow is a normal and very healthy human emotion. At some point though, you have to ask yourself: "How much is enough?" When I finally sat down and thought about it, I realised I was already making the annual income that I needed for my family's lifestyle. So, all the growth that my business goes through in the future is not really for me anymore. I have enough. It's for the team, or to be able to help more people in a life-changing way. By realising this, I was able to let go of my own tendency towards overdrive.

Life is so much more relaxed once you've asked and answered these questions for yourself. You slow down, you focus on the more important things, and you remember there are priorities outside of your business worth focusing on. For example, I intended to write this book about six months ago, and if I'd kept the same mindset I used to have, I would have pushed it out relentlessly on schedule just to not let myself down, but exhausting myself and ignoring my family in the process. However, with my new healthier, less-achievement-obsessed mindset, I instead thought, "No, writing this is not that urgent."

Acknowledging my own fears and how they drive me when left unchecked helps me relax a lot more in life than I used to.

Evaluate Why You're Working

What I also realised through a lot of hard-fought introspection is that much of what I was trying to do was to prove to my parents and to the people I used to work for that I can make it in life despite them all trying to talk me out of doing what I do. We have all got them in our lives— the people who told you to play it safe, to steer clear of entrepreneurship and follow a safe, unadventurous path in life. Did you have those people in your life as well? Years ago, a lot of people told me, "Don't start this business. It will be hard, and in the end, you won't even succeed." Now my business is huge. No one in their right mind would say I haven't succeeded. Yet, I still had to face that part of me trying to prove myself to them, saying "See, you were wrong. I did have what it takes, you know? Ta-dah! Have a look. Validate me." If you're motivated to do something for the benefit of someone else watching, you've already missed the point. What a heartbreaking motive! What an ineffective motive! Your work has to be for you to be pleasing yourself, not all about you impressing others.

You've probably realised by now there are a lot of factors that play into having a healthy business life and being a success at home too (instead of sleeping in the doghouse). We have to keep everything on track: business issues, home issues, work being too demanding, your partner being too demanding, and always asking yourself:

"What am I pushing myself so hard for?"

"What am I doing?"

"Who am I working so hard for?"

We need to ask ourselves questions like that. Do we really ever learn to deal with this stuff properly?

It's hard to do it on our own. You'll probably need a couple of mentors or maybe a life coach. I have a life coach who asks me the hard questions every fortnight:

"What are you doing with your time?"

"What's working for you and what isn't?"

"What are your motives?" "Why do you do this?"

"Why are you putting time into this?"

"You're saying these are your goals so which one will you focus on?" Those are the sorts of questions a good life coach will encourage you to reflect on, and out of it, you will achieve clarity. You will walk away and realise that you can't work with 47 priorities; you only hit a few at a time in the end.

It doesn't matter what technique or mechanism you're using to reflect on those deeper issues. Just get some clarity on them because unless you do, you will be stuck indefinitely. Your business life may improve, but you won't improve inside. Or your home life may seem a lot easier because you're working a bit less, but that part of you inside is still dealing with the same issues you don't need to be dealing with.

Next Steps: Actions Speak Louder than Plans

So, where to now? Most of what we have covered so far came from things I've learned the hard way through a series of stupid choices—foolish, impulse-driven choices in my business that have been helpful for surviving short-term but not in the long-term. In the early days, I didn't build reliable business systems and failed to set things up for the future, so I found myself trapped as a slave to my business instead of having my business serve me. A lot of people are dealing with that, and maybe that's why you picked up this book. A lot of us run businesses that are not generating the money they should, so we're forced to do everything ourselves, unable to pay others or outsource and unsure if our own staff have proper training. It's tough, but it doesn't have to stay that way.

The strategies I've shared in this book came out of the experiences I found really tough—that I chose to work really hard in my business and sacrificed a lot to help it succeed. I chose to work longer hours, to exhaust myself. I chose to be in a spot where my wife was demanding more time from me than I could give her and my kids lacked my attention, and I was swallowing stress tablets and struggling with my health. I did all of that for a few years and **for what?**

On the other side of all that drama, I look at my life now where I play a lot of sport (usually soccer), I read a couple books a week, I'm a lot more social than I used to be and I really love my life. From where I was to where I am now took work, effort and energy, but the real change happened when I chose better strategies.

Important changes to a business or an entrepreneur lifestyle won't happen in a month, or two, but six months is a realistic timeframe to get life working and on track. I made it because I took the right steps, and I know that you can as well.

Your 7 Steps to Freedom:

1. Decide on some fresh business goals and non-work goals to work towards.
2. Improve your model, offering and pricing to make your business more profitable.
3. Set up other staff to take on more of your tasks.
4. Find an experienced strategic consultant who will help you grow.
5. Systematise your business with new procedures, documented processes and better software.

6. Clarify and tighten your customer and staff policies.
7. Enjoy your business and your life a whole lot more.

Are You Ready to Grow the Next Level?

Talk to me - I'm a real person.

I'd accomplished what I'd set out to do in my tutoring business, and it hums along nicely which has freed up a lot of time for me to pursue my other passions. So now I work with business owners just like you to help them increase their profitability and get their free time back. I created About To Fly as a strategic business coaching experience for entrepreneurs and business owners.

What makes About To Fly different from every other consulting group is that I help business owners break free from the stranglehold their business has over their time and their lives. Do you see why that's so important?

I have different ways of helping businesses of almost any size. Whatever your business size is, there are always ways I can help you make more money, work a whole lot less, and enjoy your life a whole lot more.

Your perseverance and commitment to find, buy, and finish reading a book like this reflects your "can-do" attitude and rock-solid character as a business owner.

Just for you—because you made it to the end of the book and journeyed through some challenging issues and a bit of soul searching — here's a secret...

Tell me when you send a message that "I read the full book". If you do that, I've got something extra special for you to ensure you get my absolute best strategic help.

So take action now—get some extra value from About To Fly. It's easy—just go to www.abouttofly.com to book a FREE 20-minute strategy session.

About the Author

Michael Guy Clark's unconventional business strategies are simultaneously loved by practical business-owners and hated by academic-types who don't think "outside the box." After an adventurous career as a school teacher, he built and now runs Big Improvements Tutoring which disrupted the industry in two major cities and now helps kids in ten locations.

He also created About To Fly which is a unique business profitability lab, supporting niche businesses in tough industries.

If a genie would grant him one wish for his clients and other business owners, it would be to give them the knowledge of how to structure their business to run effectively and profitably without the owners' constant input. Due to the lack of genies, he wrote this book to help instead.

Michael enjoys bike-riding with his fun-loving wife and jumping on the trampoline with his two energetic kids.

How to Order

You may order this book direct from Amazon.com at: https://www.amazon.com/dp/B07KP9LMLY

Contact Information

I'm a real person, and just like you, I check my emails each day. I love to be surprised by feedback from former clients or people like you who read my books and get something out of them. I'll do my best to respond within a few days. If you take the time to reach out, I'll take the time to reply.

Michael@abouttofly.com

Amazon.com

https://www.amazon.com/dp/B07KP9LMLY

If you purchased *You're A Business Owner, Not a Slave* from Amazon.com or have an Amazon.com account, please go there and give this book a rating of up to five stars. I'd also love for you to go ahead and leave a review (takes 2 minutes). This is a big help to me and also is great for helping the right readers discover these books.

www.ingramcontent.com/pod-product-compliance
Lightning Source LLC
Chambersburg PA
CBHW021506210526
45463CB00002B/913